TEXAS A&M AGGIES

BY

MARGARET WEBER

INSIDE COLLEGE FOOTBALL

MEDIA ENHANCED BOOKS AV2 BY WEIGL ADDED VALUE • AUDIO VISUAL

www.av2books.com

Published by AV^2 by Weigl
350 5th Avenue, 59th Floor
New York, NY 10118
Website: www.av2books.com

Library of Congress Control Number: 2018968213

ISBN 978-1-7911-0123-7 (hardcover)
ISBN 978-1-7911-0124-4 (multi-user eBook)
ISBN 978-1-7911-0125-1 (single-user eBook)

Printed in Guangzhou, China
1 2 3 4 5 6 7 8 9 0 23 22 21 20 19

042019
102318

Project Coordinator: Jared Siemens   Designer: Terry Paulhus

Every reasonable effort has been made to trace ownership and to obtain permission to reprint copyright material. The publishers would be pleased to have any errors or omissions brought to their attention so that they may be corrected in subsequent printings.

The publisher acknowledges Alamy and Getty Images as its primary image suppliers for this title.

INSIDE COLLEGE FOOTBALL

Texas A&M Aggies

CONTENTS

Introduction

The Texas A&M Aggies represent Texas A&M University in National Collegiate Athletic Association (NCAA) football. Texas A&M University was formerly known as the Agricultural and Mechanical College of Texas. The nickname "Aggies" comes from that era. The Aggies play in the Southeastern Conference (SEC).

The Aggies are known for their strong traditions. The most important of these traditions is called the 12th Man. It began during a game in 1922 against Centre College, which was the number-one ranked team at that time. Due to player injuries, the Aggies had only 11 players on the field. A student named E. King Gill was part of the press covering the game. He came down from the stands to play. This spirit of student support and dedication continues today. During games, the student body stands in honor of the 12th man.

Cornerback Roney Elam played in all 6 games for the Aggies during the 2018 season. Elam logged 12 total tackles and was responsible for breaking up two passes.

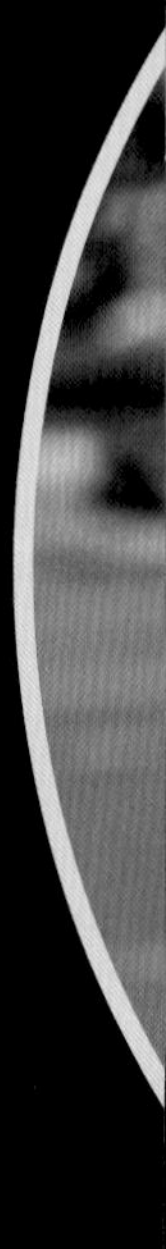

The state of Texas is also home to some of the Aggies' team **rivals**, including their number-one rival, the University of Texas Longhorns. These long-standing rivalries are popular among fans of Texas football. The Aggies first played the Longhorns the same year Texas A&M's team began. Although they have not won a National Championship in nearly 80 years, the Aggies have a strong foundation and a long history of great players and coaches that continue to push the team toward excellence.

Ben Miles spent his redshirt freshman year at the University of Nebraska before transferring to Texas A&M for the 2018 season, where he debuted as fullback against the University of Louisiana-Monroe Warhawks.

TEXAS A&M

Stadium	Kyle Field
Division	Southeastern Conference (SEC) Western
Head Coach	Jimbo Fisher
Location	College Station, Texas
National Championships	1
Nicknames	A&M, Aggies

28 Consensus All-American Players

18 Conference Championships

2 Heisman Memorial Trophy Winners

40 Bowl Games Played

History

In 1939, the Aggies had an **undefeated** season, allowing only 18 points to be scored against them during the entire regular season.

Dat Nguyen is the only linebacker in Texas A&M history to lead the team in tackles for four consecutive seasons. Nguyen led the Aggies' "Wrecking Crew" defense from 1995 to 1998.

When Texas A&M was founded in 1871, it was an all-male institution. These men were required to serve in the Corps of Cadets. In 1894, the university fielded its first football team. The first coach was F.D. Perkins. In 1919, Dana X. Bible became head coach for Texas A&M. These early coaches established a practice of excellence that continues today. Bible's very first season was undefeated, and a winning era of football began.

The Aggies continued to win in the following decades. They have won at least one conference championship in almost every decade since the 1910s. Fans have enjoyed seeing their team coached by many of college football's greatest coaches. This includes Bear Bryant, who led the team from a 1–9 season in 1954 to winning eight games in 1957.

The 1990s were an exciting time for Aggies football. The team had eight winning seasons from 1990 to 1999 under Head Coach R.C. Slocum, and won 31 home games in a row between 1990 and 1995. In 1998, they won the Big 12 Conference championship. The team did well on its home turf. Today, the Aggies are continuing these legacies with coaching **legend** Jimbo Fisher at the helm as they continue to develop into a competitive team in the SEC.

Coach Bear Bryant led the Aggies to three-straight winning seasons, a Gator Bowl appearance, and a Southwest Conference championship during his four seasons as coach.

The Stadium

Kyle Field has a 1,130-foot (340-meter) LED ribbon board. It is one of the largest in college sports. The stadium's 110-foot (34-m) screen is known as "12th Man TV."

Texas A&M University is located in College Station, Texas. The Aggies' home turf, Kyle Field, is located on campus. The team has played on these grounds since 1904, when wooden bleachers were built on an agricultural field owned by the university. In 1927, construction began on a permanent stadium. It was completed two years later.

Since 1927, there have been many improvements to the field. Expansions and construction improve both the fan and player game-time experiences. From 2013 to 2015, the stadium underwent an extensive redevelopment. The new capacity of Kyle Field became 102,733. It is one of the five largest college football stadiums in the United States. The record attendance was set during a game against the University of Mississippi Ole Miss Rebels on October 11, 2014, when 110,631 fans showed up to cheer on the Aggies.

Honoring the history of the team is a key part of Kyle Field. The Ford Hall of Champions is the largest public space on the university's campus. The Hall is a virtual museum that includes a digital display of the history of Kyle Field. A time-lapsed construction video and photos of the stadium over time are also on display in the Hall of Champions.

The 12th Man tradition at Texas A&M honors unity, loyalty, and the willingness of Aggies to serve when they are needed.

Where They Play

Welcome to Kyle Field, home of the Texas A&M Aggies. It is the largest football stadium in the SEC. It is also known as the "Home of the 12th Man." The Aggies take the field as the Corps of Cadets perform "The Aggie War Hymn." More than 100,000 loyal fans fill the seats, ready to watch their team dominate.

SEC WEST

1. **Auburn University**
   Auburn, Alabama
2. **Louisiana State University**
   Baton Rouge, Louisiana
3. **Mississippi State University**
   Starkville, Mississippi
4. ★ **Texas A&M University**
   College Station, Texas
5. **University of Alabama**
   Tuscaloosa, Alabama
6. **University of Arkansas**
   Fayetteville, Arkansas
7. **University of Mississippi**
   Oxford, Mississippi

Arena
Kyle Field

Location
College Station, Texas

Broke Ground
May 1927

Completed
September 24, 1929

Surface
Real Grass

Features
- Kyle Field is home to the A&M Sports Museum
- Named for horticulture professor Edwin Jackson Kyle, who donated and helped fund the original space for the field
- Building is 182 feet (55 m) tall at its highest point

SEC EAST

1. **University of Florida**
   Gainesville, Florida
2. **University of Georgia**
   Athens, Georgia
3. **University of Kentucky**
   Lexington, Kentucky
4. **University of Missouri**
   Columbia, Missouri
5. **University of South Carolina**
   Columbia, South Carolina
6. **University of Tennessee**
   Knoxville, Tennessee
7. **Vanderbilt University**
   Nashville, Tennessee

NORTH DAKOTA
SOUTH DAKOTA
MINNESOTA
WISCONSIN
MICHIGAN
NEW YORK
NEW HAMPSHIRE
VERMONT
MAINE
MASSACHUSETTS
RHODE ISLAND
CONNECTICUT
PENNSYLVANIA
NEW JERSEY
DELAWARE
MARYLAND
WASHINGTON, D.C.
NEBRASKA
IOWA
ILLINOIS
INDIANA
OHIO
WEST VIRGINIA
VIRGINIA
KANSAS
MISSOURI
KENTUCKY
NORTH CAROLINA
TENNESSEE
OKLAHOMA
ARKANSAS
MISSISSIPPI
ALABAMA
GEORGIA
SOUTH CAROLINA
TEXAS
LOUISIANA
FLORIDA
Atlantic Ocean
Gulf of Mexico
SCALE
0 miles
500 miles
0 kilometers
500 km
LEGEND
Home Stadium
SEC West
SEC East
United States
Other Countries
Water

The Uniforms

The "**aTm**" logo has been on the Texas A&M helmets since **1968.**

The Aggies wore special uniforms for a 2018 game against the University of Kentucky, which the Aggies won 20–14. The uniforms were a throwback to the team that took the Big 12 title in 1998.

The colors of Texas A&M are maroon and white. The typical uniform has a maroon jersey with white lettering and white pants. The away uniform is the opposite. It has a white jersey with maroon lettering and maroon pants.

In recent years, the Aggies have enjoyed playing in alternate uniforms. One example of these uniforms was worn during a game against the University of Louisiana-Monroe Warhawks on November 1, 2014. The Aggies wore special uniforms to honor the undefeated 1939 team. The maroon jerseys included wing-and-cross graphics that looked like the old helmets. The helmets the team wore were made to look like they were stitched out of leather. A stencil of the initials "AMC," to refer to the previous name of the university, the Agricultural and Mechanical College of Texas, was also on the back of the helmets. These special uniforms help remind the Aggies and its fans how far the team has come.

Before the "aTm" logo became a permanent part of the Aggies' helmets, player numbers were often displayed on the helmets. The helmet colors have most often varied between maroon and white, or a combination of the two, since 1934.

Student Athletes

At **midnight** before each home game, players and students gather for a "**midnight yell**" to build excitement before game day.

As part of the 12th Man tradition at Texas A&M, one walk-on player is selected each season to wear the number 12 jersey and take the field for "special teams plays," such as field goals or kickoff returns. Cullen Gillaspia was the Aggies' 12th man for three-straight seasons, from 2016 to 2018.

Being a college student athlete is hard work. Student athletes have to perform well on the football field and in the classroom. Texas A&M student athletes are required to meet a minimum grade point average and attend all of their classes. They must also have 12 academic credits per term.

Many student athletes are given athletic scholarships, which are financial aid agreements between the athlete and the college or university. Athletes who do not receive an athletic scholarship can be "walk-on" members of the team. This means they are on the team, but without athletic financial aid. Texas A&M typically awards the maximum number of football scholarships allowed, which is 85.

The student athletes at Texas A&M stay involved with the university even after they have graduated. In 1974, the Lettermen's Association was founded. This organization helps former student athletes return to campus to celebrate Aggie traditions. It also helps to support ongoing projects, such as improvements to Kyle Field.

Sophomore Justin Madubuike appeared in all 12 games for the Aggies in the 2018 season and was awarded the team's defensive Most Valuable Player (MVP) award for his efforts on the field.

Bowl Games

The Aggies won the **1990 Holiday Bowl** against the Brigham Young University Cougars 65–14, marking their **highest margin of victory** in a bowl game ever.

The 2018 TaxSlayer Gator Bowl was the first meeting between Texas A&M and the North Carolina State University Wolfpack. The Aggies outscored the Wolfpack 31-0 in the second half and set a Gator Bowl rushing record.

Bowl games are a unique sports tradition in college football. In the beginning of college football, there was no true **postseason**. Today, a variety of postseason bowl games are played. Bowl games give teams the opportunity to continue striving for recognition and victory after the end of regular play. There are currently 40 bowl games played in various combinations each year. These games are chosen with input from teams, sponsors, and the College Football Playoff Selection Committee. The game **matchups** are announced in December.

The Texas A&M Aggies have played in 40 bowl games. The 12th Man tradition was born during their very first bowl game, the Dixie Classic, in 1922. The Aggies defeated the Centre College Colonels 22–14. They have appeared most often in the Cotton Bowl. The Aggies have made 13 appearances in the Cotton Bowl, including three times in a row between 1992 and 1994.

Wide receiver Mike Evans had 7 receptions for 83 yards in the 2013 AT&T Cotton Bowl. Evans and the Aggies recorded 41 points against the University of Oklahoma Sooners.

The Coaches

Gene Stallings coached the Aggies from 1965 to 1971. He was 29 years old when he accepted the job, making him the **youngest** head coach in Texas A&M history.

Head Coach Jimbo Fisher's eight years at Florida State University included seven-straight winning seasons and four consecutive bowl wins. Texas A&M bought out the remainder of Fisher's contract with Florida State in order to hire him as the Aggies' head coach.

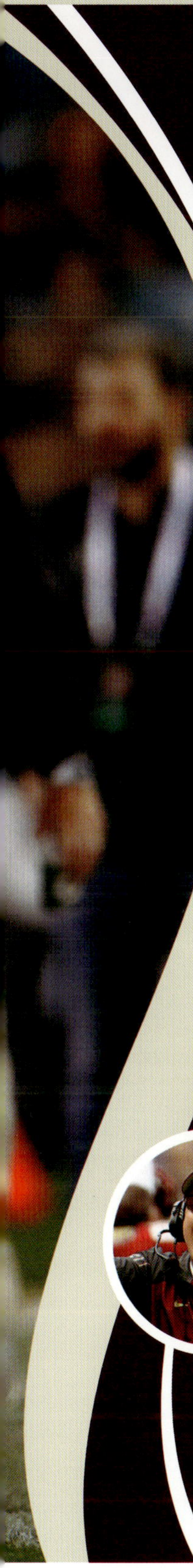

Each Aggies coach has brought new ideas and energy to the team. Some coaches, such as Harry Stiteler, were promoted to head coach after serving as a special teams coach. Others, such as Mike Sherman, came to Texas from the National Football League (NFL). Of these coaches, a few stand out for their impact on the team.

DANA X. BIBLE Dana X. Bible is well known in college football as one of the great early coaches. He coached the Aggies for 11 seasons, starting in 1917 for one season and then from 1919 to 1928. In 1917, the Aggies were undefeated and also did not surrender a single point to any opponents. In 1919, Bible led the Aggies to repeat this unbeaten season, and the Aggies finished 275–0 in total points.

R.C. SLOCUM R.C. Slocum was named head coach of the Aggies in December of 1988. He coached the team until 2002. During his tenure as head coach, the Aggies had a record of 123 total wins. He is the winningest coach in Texas A&M history. Slocum was named to the College Football **Hall of Fame** in 2012.

JIMBO FISHER Jimbo Fisher became head coach of the Aggies in December 2017. Fisher joined the Aggies from Florida State University, where he coached for eight seasons. He had a .783 winning percentage at Florida State University. That made him the winningest coach in history there. Fisher signed a 10-year contract to coach at Texas A&M. Fisher ended his first year as head coach of the Aggies with a 9–4 record and a bowl game victory.

The Mascot

Miss Rev lives with a specially designated "mascot corporal" each year and goes everywhere with him, including to class, to meals, and even on dates. The mascot corporal chosen to care for Reveille is responsible for escorting her to all Aggie functions and engagements.

Texas A&M does not have a costumed mascot. The Aggies represent their team with their mascot, Reveille IX. Reveille is a rough collie dog who comes to games and makes appearances on the field. The first Reveille was a **stray** dog found by a group of cadets in 1931. Since then, the university has carried on the tradition of having a live dog serve as its mascot. There have been nine dogs to serve in the role of Reveille.

Reveille is known as the first lady of Aggieland. Students often call her by the affectionate nickname "Miss Rev." When a Reveille dies, she is buried in a cemetery outside of Kyle Field. Reveille is considered the highest-ranking member of the Corps of Cadets. The word *réveille* means "wake up" in French and is the name of a well-known tune used to wake soldiers in the military at sunrise.

Reveille wears five diamonds on her maroon and white blanket to indicate her high rank in the Texas A&M Corps of Cadets. According to tradition, if Miss Rev decides to sleep on a cadet's bed, he has to sleep on the floor, and if she barks during a class, the rest of that class should be canceled.

Legends of the Past

For many players, their time with the Aggies is the start of a promising football career. These are some of the best-known football players to play for Texas A&M.

Von Miller

Von Miller joined the Texas A&M Aggies in 2007. He was named to the Freshman All-Big 12 team. As a sophomore, he played in all 12 games. Miller won many awards during his time in Texas, such as the Butkus Award for the nation's top linebacker. He currently plays for the Denver Broncos. He was named MVP of **Super Bowl** 50, which the Broncos won. Miller earned a poultry degree at Texas A&M and has his own farm, where he raises chickens in his free time.

Position: Defensive Lineman/Linebacker
Seasons: 2007–2010 (Texas A&M Aggies), 2011–Present (Denver Broncos)
Born: March 26, 1989, DeSoto, Texas

Ryan Tannehill

The first season Ryan Tannehill played for Texas A&M, he set a freshman record. During the fifth game of the season, he posted 210 yards on 12 catches. During Tannehill's early years on the team, he competed for the quarterback position but was not selected. He played as a wide receiver instead. By mid-season of 2010, Tannehill won the quarterback position and started all 13 games as the team's captain. He had a total of 29 touchdowns that year. He was picked eighth overall by the Miami Dolphins in the 2012 **draft** and is the Dolphins' starting quarterback.

Position: Wide Receiver/Quarterback
Seasons: 2008–2011 (Texas A&M Aggies), 2012–Present (Miami Dolphins)
Born: July 27, 1988, Lubbock, Texas

Myles Garrett

When Myles Garrett came to play with the Aggies, he was the number-two high school **prospect** in the nation. During his first year, Garrett was named a consensus Freshman All-American. In his junior year, Garrett suffered injuries that threatened to take him off the field. After sitting out two games, he returned and was named a unanimous consensus All-American for the 2016 season. In 2017, Garrett entered the NFL draft instead of continuing with his senior year. He was the number-one draft pick and was selected by the Cleveland Browns, where he remains a part of Cleveland's defensive line.

Position: Defensive Lineman
Seasons: 2014–2016 (Texas A&M Aggies), 2017–Present (Cleveland Browns)
Born: December 29, 1995, Arlington, Texas

Jake Matthews

In 2010, Jake Matthews joined the Texas A&M Aggies. Matthews came from a long line of football players. His great-grandfather, grandfather, father, uncle, two brothers, and two cousins have all been members of the NFL. Matthews played right tackle for the first three years of his career in Texas. He won recognition when he was named first-team All-SEC during his junior year. He was also awarded All-American honors. Matthews switched to left tackle in his senior year. After the 2013 season, he entered the NFL draft and was selected sixth overall by the Atlanta Falcons.

Position: Offensive Lineman
Seasons: 2010–2013 (Texas A&M Aggies), 2014–Present (Atlanta Falcons)
Born: February 11, 1992, Missouri City, Texas

All-Time Records

97
Longest Run
On November 21, 2009, Christine Michael set the record for longest run in Aggies history when he ran for 97 yards against the Baylor University Bears.

13
Single-Season Touchdowns
Josh Reynolds made 13 touchdowns in 2014, the highest number in Texas A&M history for a single season.

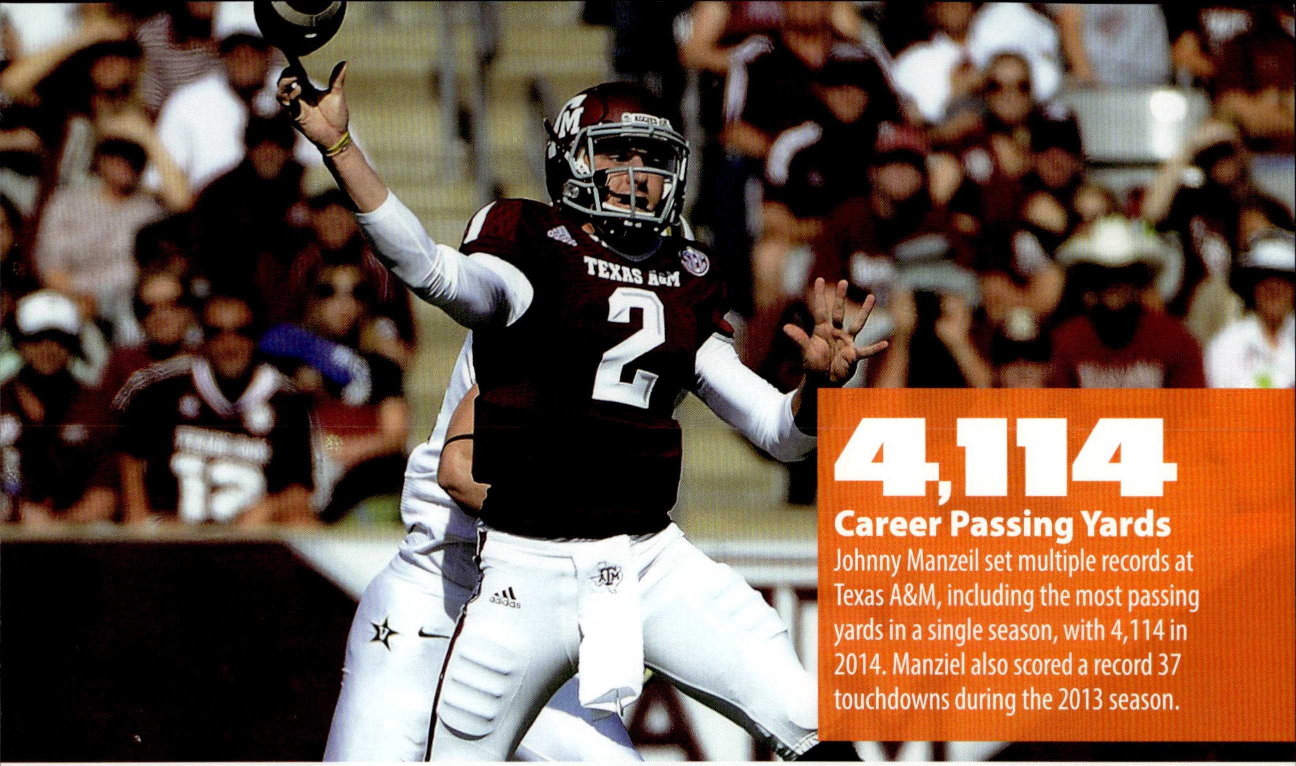

4,114

Career Passing Yards

Johnny Manzeil set multiple records at Texas A&M, including the most passing yards in a single season, with 4,114 in 2014. Manziel also scored a record 37 touchdowns during the 2013 season.

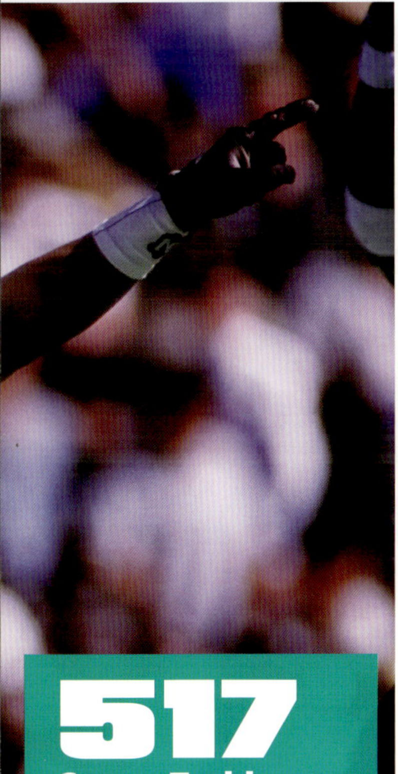

517

Career Tackles

Linebacker Dat Nguyen recorded 517 tackles from 1995 to 1998, a Texas A&M career record.

252

Career Receptions

From 2009 to 2012, wide receiver Ryan Swope set the Texas A&M record for career receptions, with 252. Swope logged a career total of 3,117 receiving yards, also a Texas A&M record.

Throughout the team's history, the Texas A&M Aggies have had many memorable events that have become defining moments for the team and its fans.

1894
The first football team in Texas A&M history takes the field.

1894
On October 19, the Texas A&M Aggies play the Texas Longhorns for the first time, starting one of the oldest rivalries in college football.

1900 | 1920 | 1940 | 1960

The Aggies see their first undefeated season in 1919.

1922
The Dixie Classic marks one of the most important games in Aggies history, as the 12th Man tradition begins.

1954
The legendary football coach Bear Bryant comes to College Station, Texas, to coach the Aggies.

1965
Gene Stallings, a coach who worked as an assistant to Bear Bryant, brings his skills and leadership to Texas A&M as head coach.

The Future

For fans in College Station and across Texas, it is an exciting time to root for the Aggies. Texas A&M has always looked to its past to guide it forward. Many strong traditions ground the team, and Coach Fisher's years of experience propel the Aggies toward championships and wins. The Aggies will bring this winning combination to their future seasons.

1988

R.C. Slocum moves from defensive coordinator for the Aggies to the position of head coach.

Kevin Sumlin, the first African American coach of the Aggies, joins the team on December 10, 2011.

1980 — 2000 — 2020

1990–1999

The Aggies only lose four home games at Kyle Field.

2018

On December 31, Jimbo Fisher leads the Aggies to a 9–4 season, including a Gator Bowl win, during his first season as head coach.

2003

On October 11, the Aggies beat the Baylor University Bears 73–10, the largest margin of victory ever in a game between the two rival teams.

Write a Biography

Life Story

A person's life story can be the subject of a book. This kind of book is called a biography. Biographies often describe the lives of people who have achieved great success. These people may be alive today, or they may have lived many years ago. Reading a biography can help you learn more about a great person.

Get the Facts

Use this book, and research in the library and on the internet, to find out more about your favorite player. Learn as much about him as you can. What position does he play? What are his statistics in important categories? Has he set any records? Also, be sure to write down key events in the person's life. What was his childhood like? What has he accomplished off the field? Is there anything else that makes this person special or unusual?

Use the Concept Web

A concept web is a useful research tool. Read the questions in the concept web on the following page. Answer the questions in your notebook. Your answers will help you write a biography.

Concept Web

Write a Biography

Adulthood
- Where does this individual currently reside?
- Does he have a family?

Your Opinion
- What did you learn from the books you read in your research?
- Would you suggest these books to others?
- Was anything missing from these books?

Childhood
- Where and when was he born?
- Describe his parents, siblings, and friends.
- Did he grow up in unusual circumstances?

Accomplishments off the Field
- What is this person's life's work?
- Has he received awards or recognition for accomplishments?
- How have this person's accomplishments served others?

Help and Obstacles
- Did this individual have a positive attitude?
- Did he receive help from others?
- Did this person have a mentor?
- Did this person face any hardships?
- If so, how were the hardships overcome?

Accomplishments on the Field
- What records does this person hold?
- What key games and plays have defined his career?
- What are his stats in categories important to his position?

Work and Preparation
- What was this person's education?
- What was his work experience?
- How does this person work?
- What is the process he uses?

Trivia Time

Take this quiz to test your knowledge of the Texas A&M Aggies.
The answers are printed upside down under each question.

1 What is the name of the stadium where the Aggies play?

A. Kyle Field

2 What is the name of the Aggies' number-one rival?

A. The Texas Longhorns

3 How many Aggies football players have won Heisman Trophies?

A. 2

4 How many times has Texas A&M appeared in a bowl game?

A. 40

5 In what year did the Aggies go undefeated and allow only 18 points to be scored against them?

A. 1939

6 What colors do the Aggies wear?

A. Maroon and white

7 In what year did the "aTm" logo first appear on players' helmets?

A. 1968

8 What was the score of the Holiday Bowl in 1990 and who did the Aggies play?

A. The Aggies won against the Brigham Young University Cougars 65–14.

9 What is the name of the mascot that represents the Aggies?

A. Reveille

10 Which former Aggie graduated with a poultry degree from Texas A&M?

A. Von Miller

Key Words

draft: an annual event where the NFL chooses college football players to be new team members

Hall of Fame: a group of persons judged to be outstanding in a particular sport

legend: an extremely well-known or famous person

matchups: contests between two athletes or sports teams

postseason: a sporting event that takes place after the end of the regular season

prospect: a player who is likely to succeed in a sport at a high level

rivals: groups or individuals who compete toward the same objective or goal

stray: an animal that does not have a home

Super Bowl: the NFL's annual championship game between the winning team from the National Football Conference and the winning team from the American Football Conference

Index

Log on to www.av2books.com

AV² by Weigl brings you media enhanced books that support active learning. Go to www.av2books.com, and enter the special code found on page 2 of this book. You will gain access to enriched and enhanced content that supplements and complements this book. Content includes video, audio, weblinks, quizzes, a slideshow, and activities.

AV² Online Navigation

AV² was built to bridge the gap between print and digital. We encourage you to tell us what you like and what you want to see in the future.

Sign up to be an AV² Ambassador at www.av2books.com/ambassador.

Due to the dynamic nature of the internet, some of the URLs and activities provided as part of AV² by Weigl may have changed or ceased to exist. AV² by Weigl accepts no responsibility for any such changes. All media enhanced books are regularly monitored to update addresses and sites in a timely manner. Contact AV² by Weigl at 1-866-649-3445 or av2books@weigl.com with any questions, comments, or feedback.